Edwin Gerard Hamamdjian

ACABI'S ARMENIAN

Idioms and popular expressions in Old Western Armenian

Illustrations by
NADIA BRUGNARA

TABLE OF CONTENTS

FOREWORD

"To see Turkish as a pollutant and to try to eliminate all traces of the language from colloquial Armenian is to ignore the historical lineage of the Armenian people."

Jennifer Manoukian,
in *The Legacy of Turkish in the Armenian Diaspora*

Why this book?

This lexicon is not meant to be a teaching manual for students wishing to learn standard Armenian, nor an exhaustive linguistic analysis of an Armenian dialect. My intention is to leave a written trace of what was once a widely used and highly expressive form of colloquial Armenian, a linguistic memoir of sorts, designed to evoke recollections, nostalgia, and a bit of humor among those who remember or still speak it. For several months, I combed through my long-term memory to compile my earliest memories of the words, expressions, and sayings that I heard throughout my childhood and which endure to this day as vivid echoes not only in my mind but in my heart.

Who was Acabi?

What is it? A language? A dialect? An idiolect?

Linguists will surely differ on how to classify it. "Acabi's Armenian," is what I chose to name this particular dialect of Western Armenian -- the first language I heard spoken and the first words I uttered.

Acabi Hamamdjian-Maurer was my maternal great-grandmother. Born in 1882 in Constantinople, she spoke a hybrid form of Turkish-Armenian, or *Dajkahayeren*, which included a hefty share of Turkish, Greek, Italian,

Acabi and her family. Constantinople. Ca. 1905

Kurdish, and Arabic loan words. It fused two completely unrelated grammatical structures from two distinct language families: one Indo-European (Armenian) and the other, Altaic (Turkish). During my childhood and early teens, 'Neneh' Acabi was alive and part of our household, consisting of my sister, parents, grandparents – (Acabi's daughter and son-in-law), and myself. Hers was the Armenian we all spoke, alternating with French and English.

Over the years American English became our predominant language of communication, and with its increased use, our cultural values and perceptions changed considerably. By the time I reached adulthood, English had almost completely replaced Armenian in our home. When I was sixteen, Acabi left this world, perhaps to continue chatting in her native dialect on the other side with friends and relatives she had outlived. I was privileged to have had, all the way into my teens, a vivacious and loquacious great-grandmother. It gave me enough years to fully absorb the sayings, images, and unique musical cadences of her colorful speech.

Nationalism, and linguistic "legitimacy"

Members of the diaspora who attended Armenian schools soon learned to eliminate all words of foreign derivation from their daily speech. There was a reason for that.

After suffering sporadic massacres in the Ottoman Empire, culminating in the genocide of 1915, the Armenian intelligentsia's need to "purify" the language by returning to its linguistic roots is wholly understandable. Since that time, well-meaning Armenian intellectuals have declared war on hybrid Armeno-Turkish, or Dajkahayeren, dialects.

The use of hybrid dialects of Armenian is often referred to, in the Republic of Armenia, as Barbaragan Hayeren ('barbarian Armenian'), underscoring the illegitimacy of those dialects.

Armenian schools have taught Makur ('Pure,' or 'Clean') Armenian, encouraging speakers of illegitimate dialects to discard all foreign words from their vocabulary and replace them with words of purely Armenian derivation.

Most members of the Armenian immigrant community in Los Angeles before the 1960's spoke barbaragan dialects of Armenian at home, and spoke "clean" Armenian mainly when addressing a formal audience. Acabi and her friends came from Istanbul or different parts of Western Armenia, (today's Turkey), and continued using the dialects they had spoken in their childhood. Although they came from distant and distinct regions of the Anatolian plateau, they easily understood each other. They paid lip-service to linguistic purity and minded their word choices to save face, mainly when addressing individuals more educated than themselves.

In spite of its academic "illegitimacy," my great-grandmother's dialect is still my living native language. And this is my modest attempt to preserve it from total extinction. UNESCO has declared Western Armenian to be an endangered language, soon to be spoken by no one. Hopefully, parts of it will continue to live and breathe here.

__Note:__ for help on how to pronounce the words and phrases listed, see the Pronunciation Guide at the end of the book and listen to the audio files at the address:

https://bit.ly/m/acabisarmenian

or scan this QR code with your smartphone:

GREETINGS

AND

AMENITIES

INDÓR ES?

Ինտո՞ր ես

How are you?

Most Western Armenians today say *Íntch bess es?*, for "how are you?" but the older word, *indór*, comes from the Persian, *in tor*, meaning THIS WAY.

AGHEG EM
Աղէկ եմ
I'm well

Agheg is less common than *lav*, the more currently used Armenian word meaning WELL; GOOD.

BAMMı NÈ GERTANKGOR ISHTÈ
Պամ մըն է կ'երթանք կոր իշթէ

"Hangin' in there," *or*
"Fair to middlin'" *or*
"It is what it is"
*would be the closest English
equivalents*

Literally, the phrase translates as: *"In short, it is something, we are going."*

Here we can already detect a sense of fatalism and wise acceptance of fate.

The Turkish *"ishtè"* can be best translated as *"here you go", "in short", "in a nutshell."*

It is widely used in Acabi's Armenian and can be likened to English "well…" when it introduces a phrase.

KYÖR TOPÁL GERTANK GOR, ISHTÈ

Քէօր-թօփալ կ'երթանք կոր, իշթէ

Well, we're moving along, blind and lame

HOKNÁTS TATRÁTS EM

Յոգնաց դադրաց եմ

I'm tired and worn out

SANK NANK
Սանգ նանգ
So-so

Abbreviated form of *"asang – anank"* meaning
THIS WAY - THAT WAY

SERSEMTSER EM!

Սերսեմցեր եմ

My mind is like mush!

Turkish: *sersem* = GIDDY

+ Armenian suffix *-tser em* = I HAVE BECOME

BıKHMISH EGHÁ
Պլխմիշ եղալ
I'm sick of it; fed up

Turkish: *bıkmış* = SICK OF

THE BODY

AND ITS

PARTS

GLOSSARY

Body parts most frequently mentioned in colloquial speech. When more than one word appears, the first is Armenian and the second and third word(s) are borrowed from Turkish.

KLUKH, KHAFÁ	Գլուխս, խաֆա.	Head
KÍT	Քիթ.	Nose
BERÁN	Պերան.	Mouth
ATCHK	Աչք	Eye
AGRÁ	Ակռայ	Tooth
LEZÚ	Լեզու	Tongue
TSERK	Ձեռք	Arm
MAD	Մատ	Finger
TEV	Թեւ	Arm
MÈMÈ	մեմե	Breast
PORR	Փոր	Belly
VORR, DIP, DIBIK	Ոռ, Տիք, Տիպիկ	Bottom
GOGOVNÉR	Կոկովներ	Testicles
SRUNK, BAJAKH	Սրունք, պաճախ.	Leg
VOTK	Ոտք	Foot

VRAN YARA YARA EGHERÈ

Վրան եարա եարա եղեր է:

On him 'wound-wound' has happened

He's hurt himself all over his body; he's seriously wounded.

Turkish: *yara* = WOUND

BEDK È TCHOOR TAPEM
Պէտք է ջուր թափեմ
I need to spill water

Meaning, 'I need to urinate.'

Armenian:
bedk è = IT IS NECESSARY
tchoor = WATER
tapem = I SPILL

BETK È SHıREM
Պէտք է շռեմ
I need to spread water (urinate)

Armenian: *shırem* = I SPREAD (WATER).

HORı KITEN INGERÈ

Հօրը գիթէն ինկեր է

She/He's dropped out of their father's nose

Meaning the child totally resembles the father, either physically or behaviorally.

Cf. "The apple doesn't fall far from the tree."

CHiGHERiS TULTSÁN
Զղերս թուլցան։
My nerves are all loose

Indicates the speaker has lost all stamina.

VOTKıT BAKNEM!

Ոտքդ պագնեմ

I kiss your foot!

This is again a hyperbolic preface to a request for a favor, similar to "If you please," or "I beg of you."

It can also be used as an ironic commentary about a person or a thing that has gone too far.

Cf. English slang interjection *"Puh-leeeeze!"*

AS PISBOGHAZUTYUN È!

Ասֆիս պոռագզություն է

This is gluttony!

as = THIS (Istanbul dialect)

Turkish: *pis* = DIRTY; *boghaz* = THROAT.

Pis-boghaz-utyun = DIRTY THROAT-NESS.

When someone overeats, you can admonish them by saying "This is dirty-throat-ness."

KITı-BERANı KEDINı ZARGÁV!

Քիթը բերանը գետինը զարկաւ

His NOSE - his MOUTH hit the ground!

The 'nose-mouth' are synecdoche for the whole body when referring to injuries, falls, accidents or any form of physical violence that a person may sustain.

NEVAZIL OUNI
Նեւազիլ ունի
He/She has a cold

Turkish: *nevazil* = COMMON COLD

GOGOVNERıS URETZUTS!
Կոկովներս ունեցուց
He/She swelled my balls!

Refers to the physical effect of a tiresome person who rants on and on about a subject of no interest.

Variant:

AGANCHNÉRIS URETZUTS!
Ականջներս ունեցուց
He/She swelled my ears!

HAST KHAFÁ! (INAT)
Հաստ խաֆա (ինատ)
A thick head (stubborn)

ALTıKH SIRDıS HADÁV

Ալթըխ սիրտս հատաւ

I'm emotionally drained!

Literally: "My heart ran out."

Altıkh is a variation on Turkish: *artık* = BY NOW; NO LONGER.

This expression is very close to *Bıkhmísh eghá* (see above), but rather than being fed up of something someone else is doing, here you've worn your heart out attempting to do something yourself... like trying to convince your eleven-year old to tidy her room, or spending hours trying to get some bureaucrat at the Hall of Records to answer their phone.

ANOR ANGATCH MÍ GAKHER!
Անոր անկաջ մի կախեր
Don't listen to him!

Literally: "Don't hang your ear on him."

Angatch = variation on *aganch* = EAR (Istanbul dialect)

SOME

OFT-MENTIONED

FOODS

GLOSSARY

Again, where several words appear, the first one is Armenian and the second is Turkish. I include both, because Acabi and her daughter used them interchangeably.

BANANESS	Պանանես	Banana
PATATESS	Փաթաթես	Potato
DOMATESS	Տոմադես	Tomato
VARUNK, KHIYAR	Վարունգ, Խիար	Cucumber
HÁTS	Հաց	Bread
PANÍR	Պանիր	Cheese
ABÚR	Ապուր	Soup
TıTÚM, KHABÁKH	Դդում, խապախ	Zucchini, Squash
SEKH, KHAVÚN	Սեխ, խավուն	Melon
TSMERÚK, KHARPÚZ	Ձմերուկ, խարբուզ	Watermelon
KHAVOGH (KHAGHOGH)	Խավող (խաղող)	Grapes
MEES	Միս	Meat
HAVGÍT	Հավկիթ	Eggs
MAKHARNÁ	Մախառնա	Pasta (both macaroni and spaghetti)
TEY, CHAY	Թէյ, չայ	Tea
SURJ, KHÁKHVÈ	Սուրճ, խախվէ	Coffee

BANIR-HATS
պանիր-hաց
Cheese-bread

The two went together as a frequent snack. There was no need to connect them with "and."

Often the word *PɪSHɪR* was added to indicate a small portion, giving us the expression:

PɪSHɪR Mɪ BANIR-HATS
Փշըր մը պանիր-hաց
A bit of cheese and bread

FıSHıR FıSHıR MAKHARNÁ
Ֆըշըր Ֆըշըր մախարնա
'Sizzling' spaghetti

The Italian influence was very strong in Constantinople, and pasta was an important part of our diet, especially after my family moved to the States. The Turkish adjective *fişir fişir*, translated as effervescent, can be used here to describe the sizzling sound of pasta tossed in a saucepan when being warmed up for a late-night snack. Acabi and her children and grandchildren (meaning all of us), frequently craved the comfort of a late, warm plate of pasta before bedtime. It helped us sleep better, believe it or not.

KHɪRT PɪRT; KHɪVɪR ZɪVɪR
Խըրթ-փըրթ, խըվըր-զըվըր
A bit of this, a bit of that / Odds and ends

When there was no major meal planned, the family would dine on various leftovers and tidbits. Acabi would say "We're having *khɪrt-pɪrt* for dinner." Another variant was "We're having *khɪvɪr zɪvɪr.*"

A variant on the same theme was ***DAKTSÚR PAKTSÚR*** տաքցուր բաքցուր, literally *Warm it, Stick it…* meaning 'warm it up and stick it on the table.' When unexpected people showed up at lunch or dinnertime and there wasn't enough to go around, and this happened quite regularly, we would heat up whatever odds and ends we could find and improvised a meal.

Throughout my childhood, and long before people ordered last-minute home deliveries, there was a continuous stream of Armenian immigrants arriving in California who'd somehow end up at our house. Usually nephews and sometimes nieces of my parents or grandparents. Some of them stayed for months, even years, attending college, learning English, while waiting for their visas and citizenship papers to be processed.

KıTıR HÁTS

Քրթըր hաց

Cracker bread

The onomatopoeia *kıtır* refers to the crunching sound made when biting into a cracker or a dry crust of bread. Seemed like there were always breadsticks and crispy bits of dried pita or *ak-mak* in the kitchen when Acabi was around. These were always available to help fill the stomach during those scanty *khıvır zıvır* dinners.

BAGHADZABOUR
Պաղածապուր
Soup gone cold

To characterize someone as "cold soup" simply means they're boring.

KHABAKHÍ HÁMM GOODAS GOR!

Խապախիի համ կուտաս կոր

You're starting to taste like zucchini!

A common complaint when a person goes on and on about a given subject.

The premise is that nothing tastes blander than zucchini. The message is he/she would do well to stop repeating the same thing and change the subject.

Turkish: *khabakh* = ZUCCHINI, or SQUASH.

Armenian: *hámm* = TASTE / *goodas-gor* = YOU ARE GIVING

Also there is the Armenian word *tıtoom* = SQUASH

As with most of these expressions, one can use the Armenian equivalent: **"Tıtoomí ham goodas-gor."**

This phrase brings to mind Oscar Wilde's famous line: "Like all people who try to exhaust a subject, he exhausted his listeners."

QUIPS
AND
PUTDOWNS

...and there are a lot of them!

Many put-downs in Acabi's Armenian end with the phrase:

BAM Mı NÈ

Պամ մըն է

...is something...

Bam mı nè is Acabi's pronunciation of *pan mı nè* in classical Western Armenian.

Pan = THING; *mı* = the indefinite article "A", always comes after the noun.

When placed after a noun or adjective, *bam mı nè* best translates as "Is something of a ..."

Some examples are listed in the following pages.

KHAYıRSıZ BAM Mı NÈ

Խայլրրսրզ պամ մրն է

He's something of a brazen,
unapologetic person

ZAVALı BAM Mı NÈ

Զաւալը պամ մըն է

She's a poor, unfortunate soul

KHEGHJU GURAK BAM Mı NÈ

Խեղճ-կրակ պամ մըն է

He/She's a pathetic thing

Literally 'A poor, blind thing...' as *gurak* can also mean BLIND. However, they can be a poor, blind thing in the figurative sense of one who cannot see how pathetic he/she is.

HANÁDZ VARÁDZ BAM Mı NÈ

Հաննած-վարած պամ մըն է

He/She's got a checkered past

The closest English equivalent could be "...someone who's 'been around.'"

Armenian: *hanadz* = TAKEN OUT; *varadz* = IGNITED, as in 'turned on.'

A condescending way to sum up a person's moral reputation, usually sexual.

Variant:

ARADZ KATSADZ BAM MI NÈ

Առած-գացած պամ մըն է

KHAKHALOZ BAM Mı NÈ

Խախալող պաս մրն է

He's an oaf, a simpleton

BAMMı NAL TCHIHASıKNAR
Պամ մըն ալ չի հասկնար
She doesn't understand a thing

Literally: "A thing also (he) doesn't understand."

SURATSıZ MEK NÈ
Սուրաթսրզ մէգն է
He/She's a faceless one

To be faceless here means unabashed; one who does what one pleases without caring how it is seen by others.

Turkish: *surat* = FACE

+ suffix *-sız* = WITHOUT

KHIYÁKH BAN!

Խրյախ պան

What a marvelous thing!

Khiyakh! implies something awesome or extraordinary, and can also be translated as 'Wow!"   In Acabi's language, it's invariably used sarcastically, to put something or someone down. Similar to English 'Big deal!"

Cf. **SÖZDÈ KHIYÁKH YERKJUHI È.**
Սէօզտէ խրյախ երգճուհի է
She's supposedly a great singer!

Turkish: *sõzdè* = SUPPOSEDLY

Armenian: *yerkjuhi* = SINGER (fem.)

ÁMMA ıRÍR A!
Ա՝մմայ ըրիր այ:
Don't exaggerate!

Literally: "...You really did it!"

Turkish: *amma* = BUT, used here to mean 'really'

Armenian: *ırir* = YOU DID

Ah! = a widely used particle of emphasis at the end of a phrase. Variant: *Ya!* origin could be Persian or even Armenian dialectical variation of *È* (is). *"A!"* and *"Ya!"* are never accented in speech. The stress is placed on the syllable immediately preceding the particle.

This expression is used to inform someone that he/she is grossly exaggerating.

Example:

A: "You were on the phone for one hour with Ani!" *B:* "One HOUR ?? *Amma ırír ah!* We barely spoke fifteen minutes!"

TSɪNTER È

Ցնդեր է

He/She has "disappeared"

A euphemism for "...gone senile".

SATKÍ NÈ HÓKıS CHÈ!

Uաղկի նե hոqu չէ

...can drop dead for all I care

KHELATSÍ GARABED!
Խելացի Կարապետ
Clever Garabed!

Khelatsí = SMART, CLEVER

Garabed = A MAN'S NAME

'Clever Garabed' is the Armenian equivalent of 'Simple Simon!' and should be interpreted as meaning that the person referred to is the exact opposite of clever.

SARSÁKH MUSTAFÁ!
Սարսախ մուսթաֆա
Silly Mustafa!

Sarsákh = SILLY

A 'Silly Mustafa' is a silly clown!

ASOR HIYÉTı NAYÈ
Ասոր հիյէթը նայէ
Look at that getup!

Asor = HIS/HER (Istanbul dialect), literally, "of this one" (cf. *anor* = OF THAT ONE)

HASAGIN TCHAP LEZÙ UNI

Հասագին չափ լեզու ունի

He/She has a tongue as tall as their body

Characterizes someone who doesn't know how to keep their mouth shut, not to be trusted to keep a secret.

BICHIMSÍZ!
Պիչիմսիզ,
Vulgar, unkempt

BICHIMSIZ MEKN È
Պիչիմսիզ մեգն է
He/She's has no style, no taste

Variant: **BICHIM CHALıM Պիչիմ չալըմ**

KALVATSKı NAYÈ!

Քալուածքը նայէ:

Look at how he/she walks

GOVÍ BES VORı Gı KHAGHTSUNÈGOR!

կովի պէս որը կը խաղցունէ կոր

Moves like a cow's ass

To walk slowly and ploddingly, with each cheek of the ass going up and down like a see-saw.

AD GNIGı MEES OUDOGH È, HEROO GETSEK!

Ատ կնիկը միս ուտող է, հեռու կեցէք

That woman's a gossip. Stay away!

KHAZıKHÍ BES MECHDEGH ELAV!

Խազրխի պէս մէջտեղ էլաւ

He/She suddenly showed up like a stick in the ground

The phrase actually includes the Turkish word '*kazık*' meaning 'STAKE.' The image is that of some elongated object that's firmly planted in the ground and doesn't budge.

Armenian '*mechdegh*' means 'IN THE MIDDLE' and '*elav*' in this context would best be translated as 'SHOWED UP.'

A purely literal translation would be "*Like a stake in the ground, he/she showed up in our midst.*"

KAKNEM SURAT-NÍN!

Քաքնեմ սուրաթնին

May I shit on their faces!

An over-the-top expression of absolute rage.

Turkish: *surat* = FACE

-nín = Armenian 3rd person plural possessive suffix

ZEVZEK!

Զևզեկ

You silly!

ABOUSHIN MEKNÈ!
Ապուշին մէգն է
He/She's one stupid fool!

aboushín = from among the stupid

meknè (megı nè) = is ONE of them

REQUESTS

AND

INJUNCTIONS

INDZI KHADEKH Mı CHOOR BER

Ինծի խատէխ մը ջուր պեր

Bring me a glass of water

Khadekh, from the Arabic *Qdeh* meaning CUP or VESSEL. Commonly used in South-Eastern Turkish dialects.

VAZ ANTSIR

Վազ անցիր:

Skip it; give it up

From Turkish: *vaz geç* = GIVE IT UP

KHNTREM GÁRTCH GABÈ !

Խնդրեմ կարճ կապէ:

Please, make it short!

As in 'Cut to the chase!'

khntrem = PLEASE

DZUR NıSTÈ, SHIDAK KHOSÈ!
Ծուռ նստէ, շիտակ խօսէ
Sit crooked, but talk straight

This is a request for someone to stop beating around the bush, or worse, to stop being deceitful, but to speak honestly and directly.

HAMÓV HODÓV GÉR!
Համով հոտով կե՛ր
Enjoy! (to someone who's eating)

ham-óv = WITH TASTE

hod-óv = WITH AROMA, SMELL

Literally: "Eat with taste and aroma!"

KHENT ES NÈ 'KHENT EM' ıSÈ!
Խենթ ես նէ խենթ եմ ըսէ
You're out of your mind!

khent = CRAZY

Literally: "If you're crazy (*khent*), say 'I'm crazy'."

Nè (IF) follows the clause it modifies. So literally *"Khent es nè"* is translated as "If you are crazy... (say I am crazy)"

CHÍSHɪT ɪRÈ GNA BARGÈ!
Չիշդ ըրէ գնա պառկէ
Go pee and then to bed!

This peremptory command to remind the child that it's way past his/her bedtime was never part of Acabi's, or any polite lady's vocabulary. It was always more of a daddy thing.

MEZI MASAL MÍ BATMER!
Մեզի մասալ մի պադմեր
Don't tell us tales!

When a parent suspects their child is lying or fibbing, this command confirms they're not buying it. It can also be directed to adults, especially when someone seems to be fishing for excuses after not keeping their word.

Can be used concurrently, or in place of, *"Dzur nıstink shidak khosink."*

TOGH KEDÍNı ANTSNÍ!
Թող գետինը անցնի
May he pass underground!

A truly rancorous expletive for a someone to simply drop dead.

ARABANÍS KASHENK?

Արապանիս քաշե՞նք

Shall we pull out our carriage?

Turkish: *araba* = CAR, CART

After a long visit, social event, or any family outing, at some point someone will say 'Shall we pull out our carriage?' meaning 'Is it time to go?'

MEG1 AR MYUSÍN ZARK!

Մէկը առ միւսին զարկ

Take one and whack him against
the other!

When having to choose between two people,
neither of whom would be a good choice, this
expression is a double put-down. Both options
are bad, so just take one and whack him
against the other!

This could apply, for example, to two suitors, two actors, two professors, two students, or even two presidential candidates!

Variant: *Megı ar megalín zark!*

Acabi often used the Greek *Megál* interchangeably with Armenian *Myus* to mean OTHER.

AS KEZI GÖRÈ BAN CHÈ!

Աս քեզի կէօրէ պան չէ

This does not concern you/
Mind your own business!

Turkish: *göre* = REGARDING

Literally, "This is not a 'you-regarding' thing".

Variant: **AYS KOU KORDZIT TCHÈ այս քու գործդ չէ** This is not your business.

Armenian: *kordz* = WORK

ASI CH'ıLLAR!
Ասի (ասիկա) չըլլար
This mustn't be!

To express one's opposition to an action or situation.

Literally translated as the closest common English equivalent "this is not OK!"

TCHAPı MI ANTSUNER!
Չափը մի անցունէր
Don't overdo it!

Basically this is to tell someone to hold back a bit, they've gone too far or too long: eating, talking, exercising, or practicing the trombone.

DESCRIBING PEOPLE

AND THEIR PERSONALITIES

SHENK SHNORKOV ERIK-MART
Շէնք շնորքով էրիքմարդ
A decent self-respecting gentleman

Armenian: *erik* = MALE, *mart* = PERSON, MAN

Depending on which side of the political spectrum you're on, a *'shenk shnorkhov'* man can either be an eligible, responsible future husband for your daughter, or a straight-laced, provincial bore.

ANKHIYEREN Gı KHOSI
Անխիիերէն կը խոսի:
He speaks English

Normally in Armenian, English is pronounced and spelled *Anklerén*, but Acabi used the variant AN-KHIYEREN.

MEES OUDOGH EN!

Միս ուտող են

These people are gossips!

Literally, "They're flesh-eaters."

People who talk about you behind your back are figuratively eating your flesh.

BABÁT VɪRAN LIMÓN Gɪ KAMÈ!
Պապադ վրան լիմոն կը քամէ
Your dad can squeeze a lemon on him!

To 'squeeze lemon' over someone denotes superiority. If you tell Eddy his father can squeeze lemon over Kenny's father, that means Eddy's dad is better, stronger, smarter than Kenny's. This way Eddy stays proud of his father.

ARATCH TOGH VARDIKı GABÈ!

Առաջ թող վարտիքը կապէ

Let him learn to tie his underpants!

Refers to a younger person who is overconfident or too proud of oneself, especially one who likes to give advice to his or her elders. Closest English equivalent: "Too big for his breeches."

Generally, it is impolite for younger Armenians to lecture or give advice to people twice or three times their age. To do so often gives way to exclaiming vociferously that this "young upstart" needs a lesson in humility.

DESCRIBING
ACTIONS
AND
EVENTS

PAT-KÜT

Փաթ-քիւթ

Slam...bang!

TCHAKH-DEYI!

Չախ տեյի

Crash ... bang!

These are onomatopoeias describing actions, specifically the sounds of objects hitting against one another. These could include pots and pans as well. The second one suggests the sound of a hand slapping a face: TCHAKH!

Pat-Küt is a contraction of Turkish *Paldır-Küldür* = HEADLONG

KITı BERANı MEKAT Mı PAGTSOOTSÍ!

Քիթը պերանը մէքատ մը փակցուցի

I stuck one to his nose-mouth!

Again, this describes the violent slapping or punching of another person. "Nose-mouth" are often paired up to indicate one's whole face. When a person falls on his or her face, the same two words express intensity of the collision.

Cf. page 32, #31.

INCH SOSKALI MARIFETNER GıNEGOR!

Սոսզալի մարիֆէթներ կ'ընէ կոր

What amazing feats he/she's performing!

I'm not sure why I'm including this phrase. Something about the Turkish word *marifèt* has always fascinated me. The Google translation of the word is "ingenuity," but somehow in Acabi's Armenian it often referred to physical feats of skill, like tumbling or gymnastics.

INCH AGHVOR PIANO "GɪTCHALÈ"

Ինչ աղուոր փիանո կը ջալէ

How well he/she plays the piano

The correct Armenian verb for playing an instrument is *nıvakel*. Acabi used the verb *tchalel*.

Pure Armenian form would be "to play the piano", *tashnak nıvakel*

LiMiNTSÁV-GiNÁTS!
Լմնցաւ կնաց
That's that! Over and done with!

Literally the phrase reads "it finished - went away."

SA BANı VURDEKHEN MECHDEGH (ORTÁN) ELÁV?

Սա պանը վուրտեխէ՛ն մէջտեղ (օրթան) էլաւ

Where did this thing come from?

Literal translation: /This thing/ from which place?/ in our midst/ came out/

This phrase is full of regional variations in pronunciation, starting with *Sa* for *Ays* = THIS; *Vurdekhén?* for *Vor deghén?* = WHICH PLACE?;

Elav for *Yelav*, the simple past of *Yellel* = TO COME UP, COME OUT.

Armenian: *mechdegh* = MIDDLE / MIDST

(*Mechdegh* can also be replaced by the Turkish *Orta*, meaning MIDDLE, to which the Armenian definite article *N* is added, giving us *ortán* = THE MIDDLE.

OORE NÈ, BIDI KAN
Ուր է նէ պիտի գան
They'll be here any minute

Literally: "Wherever it is, they are coming."

Here, 'Wherever' connotes temporality rather than location.

DA'A OOR ÈS?

Sуhш n՛ւр ես

You have a long way to go

Literally: "Still, where are you?"

Turkish: *daha*, /da'a/ = STILL
Armenian: *oor es?* = WHERE ARE YOU?

With this rhetorical question, Acabi would remind me that I was still a child and had a long way to go before thinking about driving a car, or getting married, or what I'd be when I grow up.

When used in the 3rd person singular: *"Daha oor eh?"* it can refer to anything that still requires time to complete.

Example:
Question: "Do you think the meat is cooked yet?"
Answer: *"Daha oor eh?* It still needs another hour!"

AMEN DEGH TAPTıPEL È

Ամէն տեղ թափթփեէլէ

It has spilled everywhere

Acabi's Armenian plays around with verbs by inserting random syllables in the middle of the word. For example the verb *tapel* (SPILL) becomes *tap-tı-pel* which emphasizes the messiness caused by the spilling. Similarly you can embellish other verbs to modify their meaning. For example, *shıdkel* (FIX) becomes *shıd-kır-del* (to FIX HASTILY), when the work done is a bit slapdash.

AMAN, VAKHıS INCH ER?
Ամման Վախս ի՞նչ Էր
Oh my God, what was THAT?

Literally: "What was my fear?"

Aman = OH MY GOD

This phrase meaning "What just startled me?" is uttered as an exclamation after someone has been startled by a sudden noise or crashing sound. Or simply being startled by a person, or your pet suddenly jumping on your lap.

BIRDEN BIRÈ... Պիրտէն պիրէ
MEGENI MEK... մեկէն ի մեկ
All of a sudden...

The first phrase is Turkish, literally meaning "From one to one."

Turkish: b*ir* = ONE.

The second version is Armenian, also meaning "From one to one." Armenian: m*eg* = ONE.

Acabi used both versions to express suddenness or unexpectedness.

VIRT DEYI

Վըրդ տեյի

In a jiff

Something done suddenly is done in a *'vɪrt'*, Turkish for WHIRR.

INDZI JÈHENEMÍN BUJAKHı DARAV!

Ինծի ճեհենեմին պուճախը տարաւ

He/She took me away to the furthest corner of hell!

A common complaint when one was dragged along on an endless journey. Can also be used to mean "He took me on a wild goose chase."

Turkish: j*ehenem* = HELL; b*ucak* = CORNER;

Armenian: *darav* is the 3rd person preterit form of *danel* = TO TAKE AWAY

EYLENJÈ UNETSANK
Էյլէնճէ ունեցանք
We had fun

Turkish: *eylence* = FUN.

CH'È MI?

ՉԷ՛ մի

Isn't it so?

Armenian: *ch'è* = IT ISN'T.

Turkish: *mi* = Particle placed at the end of a phrase to make it interrogative.

Then there's the opposite 'Is that so?' which would be **È MI? Է՛ մի**

ORDU HANETS
Օրտու համեց
He/She made a racket

Literally : "He/She raised an army."

Turkish: *ordu* = ARMY.

MADERıS HEDı GERAH !
Մատերս հետր կերայ
I ate my fingers with it!

This is to compliment someone's excellent cooking.

PHYSICAL SITUATIONS AND MENTAL STATES

KHiKHTiVIM BIDI!

Խխղուիմ պիտի

I'm about to choke!

The placement of the future particle *"bidi"* in Western Armenian subtly changes the subtext.

When placed before the verb, as in *bidi boram,* it means 'I'm going to scream'.

If placed after the verb, *boram bidi,* it implies greater urgency, as in 'I'm about to scream right now!'

MERNÍM BIDI!

Մեռնիմ պիտի

I'm about to die!

A common hyperbole that indicates the speaker has reached their limit of stress, fatigue... or even hysterical laughter!

CHURERÙN METCH'N È!

Ջուրերուն մէջն է

He/She is in the waters!

Indicates that someone is dripping in sweat.

DAMARıS BıRNETS
Տամարս բռնեց
I lost my temper

Literally, "My vein took hold."

Turkish: *damar* = VEIN

KHıRS ELAH

Խըրս էլայ

I got angry

CHEMKIDER INCH/BILMEMNÈ
Չեմ գիտեր ինչ/պիլմեմնէ
I haven't a clue

Both phrases, the first Armenian, the second Turkish, literally mean "I don't know what."

Both were used commonly.

FILÁN-FALÁN Ֆիլան-Ֆալան
FILÁN-FıSTıKH Ֆիլան-Ֆըսդըխ
This and that/Etcetera

Turkish: *filan falan* = SUCH AND SO...

In our dialect, *falán* was often replaced by *fıstıkh* = PISTACHIO

VÍRA NUYN KHıNTIRNÈ
Վիրա նոյն խնդիր'նե
It's always the same problem

Acabi's mysterious use of *Víra* (ALWAYS, REPEATEDLY) remains inexplicable to me. I have searched and searched but haven't yet found any plausible source word with a similar meaning in Armenian, Turkish, or Greek.

KHABAR TCHÈ!

Խապար չէ

He hasn't a clue

Turkish: *khabar* = NEWS but in this phrase it means to be aware of the news.

Armenian: *tchè* = ISN'T

MENK MEZI
Մենք մեզի
...us to ourselves

At times, after having spent days feeding and entertaining guests, Armenians prefer to keep to themselves – family only.

That's when they say, "Tonight let's keep it *menk mezi*." (AMONG OURSELVES)

KHAKHVEN TASHMISH EGHAV
Խախվեն թաշմիշ եղաւ
The coffee overflowed

Turkish (or Armenian) coffee, being an integral part of daily life in our household, it was only natural that we use the Turkish word *Taşmış* (OVERFLOW) to describe those frequent accidents where a split second of distraction would cause the coffee to spill over and send sparks flying over the dark, muddy puddles on the stovetop.

Khakhvè is the way they pronounced *kahve*, Turkish for COFFEE. Occasionally, when there was company, they'd use the Armenian word for coffee: *sourj* (**սուրճ**)

HELBET HASKıTSAN
Հելբեթ հասկցան
Of course they understood

Kurdish: *helbet* = OF COURSE; DEFINITELY

DOONı DAKNı VıRA TSıKETS
Տունը տակնը վրայ ձգեց
He left the house in a mess

Armenian: *dagı* = UNDER; *vıra* = OVER

Dag nı Vra (UNDER-OVER) = topsy-turvy; messy

Doon ı = THE HOUSE; *tsıketsín* = THEY LEFT

VAKHÍT CHUNIM
Վախիթ չունիմ
I don't have time

Turkish: *vakit* = TIME

The Armenian word for time would be "*zhamanág.*"

BARAP DEGHı YEGÁV
Պարաք տեղը Էկաւ
He/She came for nothing

Armenian: *barap* = EMPTY ; *degh* = PLACE. 'Empty place' can mean 'For nothing.'

Variation with Turkish: *boş* = EMPTY.

Boş deghı yegav. = He came for nothing.

BAM MıN AL CHıHASKıTSAV
Պամ մըն ալ չհասգցաւ
He didn't understand a thing

Literally: "A thing 'also' he didn't understand."

Armenian: *al* = ALSO. Here "also" can also mean "even."

ABUKH SUBUKH BAM MıNÈ
Ապուխ սուպուխ պամ մըն է
It's nonsense

Turkish: *abuk subuk* = NONSENSE

Gɪ NAYIS TE Կը նայիս թէ
Gɪ NAYIS KI Կը նայիս քի
+ action...

they just might... (don't be surprised if...)

Ex: **Gɪ NAYIS KI SHUNɪ HEDERNIN Gɪ BEREN.**
Կը նայիս քի շունը հետերնին պիտի պերեն

Don't be surprised if they bring their dog.

Literally: "You will see that (she will bring her dog along)." Here, "You'll see that..." works as a caveat.

Armenian: *Gɪ nayis ki* = YOU'LL SEE THAT...

ki = THAT

The verb *naél* can mean both LOOK and SEE. The phrase, prefaced by the words "you'll look (see) that..." suggests that something you don't wish to happen might very well happen.

ALTıKH TCHAPı ANTSÚTS
Ալդըն չափը անցուց
In the end, she went too far

Literally: "She surpassed the limits."

In Acabi's Armenian, the Turkish *Artık* (FINALLY) is pronounced *Altıkh*.

KAKı GUERÁV!

Քաքը կերաւ

He ate the shit!

Refers to a person who's got him/herself into trouble.

PLACES

AND

OBJECTS

DAJÍK Տաճիկ Turk, Turkic

DAJKASTÁN Տաճկաստան
Turkey, Azerbaïjan, any Turkic speaking region

DAJKAHÁY Տաճկահայ
A Western Armenian, an Armenian coming from Anatolia or any part of modern-day Turkey. (Synonym: "Turkahay")

DAJKAHAY ERÉN Տաճկահայերեն
The Western-Armenian or Turkish-Armenian language

Whenever Acabi talked about Turkey and Turkish people, she rarely used the word Türk, the official Armenian name for that ethnicity, but rather an older name for Turks, Dajik, which, ironically, refers to the only Central Asian republic that does NOT speak a Turkic language. Oddly enough, the word Dajik is the voiced variant of the T in Tajik, the official language of Tajikistan. The Tajiks speak a dialect of Persian, which is an Indo-European as opposed to a Turkic language.

It is actually quite remarkable that with all the Turkic-speaking peoples in the region, including Kazakhs, Uzbeks, Azeris, Turkmens, Kyrghyz, to name a few, Armenians chose the one non-Turkic speaking group to refer to all Turks.

BOLÍS Պոլիս
Istanbul, Constantinople

BOLSETSÍ Պոլսեցի
An inhabitant of Istanbul

BOLSAHÁY Պոլսահայ
An Armenian from Istanbul

BOLSAHAYERÉN Պոլսահայերեն
The Istanbul dialect of Armenian

Bolis is the Armenian pronunciation for none other than the Greek word *Polis* = CITY.

And to most Armenians during the Ottoman times, Constantinople was indeed the capital of the Empire and the quintessential "CITY." Armenians were sent there by their families from all over Anatolia to study, achieve success, and realize their potential. Armenians who were permanently settled there contributed greatly to the architectural, artistic and intellectual marvels that have made Bolis one of the world's most beautiful cities.

DUNı MAS MAKUR È

Տունը մաս-մաքուր է

The house is spotless

Makur = CLEAN; *Mas makur* = TOTALLY CLEAN

As in many words in our dialect, the emphatic form of an adjective uses the first syllable of the adjective and changes its final letter to intensify the quality described by the adjective.

Example: MAK(our) => MAS. The K is replaced by an S. To go from CLEAN to VERY CLEAN, you say MAS before MAKOUR, which makes it SPOTLESS.

The same process, borrowed from Turkish grammar, is used to describe the intensity of COLORS.

Examples (Color) :

GARMÍR կարմիր Red

> **GÁS GARMÍR** Կաս-կարմիր
> Bright red

GABÚYT կապույտ Blue

> **GÁP GABÚYT** Կապ կապույտ
> Bright blue

TEGHÍN դեղին Yellow

> **TEP TEGHÍN** Դեփ-դեղին
> Bright yellow

GANÁNCH կապույտ Green

> **GÁP GANÁNCH** Կապ-կապույտ
> Bright green

JERMÁG ճերմակ White

> **JEP JERMAG** Ճեփ-ճերմակ
> Very white

SEV սեւ Black

> **SEP SEV** Սեփ-սեւ Very black

Other examples:

TÁTS **թաց** Wet

TÁP TÁTS **Թափ-թաց**
Very wet

NOR **նոր** New

NOP NOR **Նովզ-նոր**
Brand new

[variant: **NOPIZ NOR** Brand New]
...don't ask me where that bizarre
variant came from !

BILLORI BES
Պիլլորի պէս
(It's shining) like crystal, brilliant

Cf. Arabic : *bilora* = CRYSTAL

VOTKÍ AMANNÉRıS
Ոդքի ամաններս
My shoes

Literally: "My 'foot pots.'"

KHUTIÍN METCHı DIR
Խուդիին մէչը տիր
Put it in the box

Turkish: *kutu* = BOX, becomes *khutí*

[Compare with Turkish *kuzu* = LAMB, becomes *khuzí* (խուզի) meaning "lamb", in Acabi's Armenian.]

COMPLAINTS

INDZI DOGH MI HANER !

ինձի առդ մի հաներ

Don't scare me! Don't get me worried...

Literally: "Don't get me startled!"

DAHA BETÈR
Տահա պեթէր
Even worse

Oddly enough, Turkish: *betèr* = WORSE

MOOKHıS MARETSÁV
Մուխս մարեցաւ
I'm wiped out

Literally: "My smoke's been extinguished."

ÍLLÈ INKE GUZÈGOR VDJARÈL
Իլլէ ինքը պէտք է վճարէ
He wants to pay at all cost

When a person is dead-set on doing something, you can express your disapproval with *Íll*è, Turkish for NECESSARILY.

KHAFÁS URETZÚTZ

Խաֆաս ուռեցուց

He/She made my head swell up

Refers to someone who talks way too much.

Turkish: k*hafá* = HEAD. + /S/ the possessive suffix 'my.'

ONDÁNDıR
Օնտաննարը
It's from 'that'...

I would often hear elderly ladies and gentlemen complaining to Acabi about their various aches and pains. The euphemism *"Ondándir"* = IT'S FROM 'THAT' was the automatic reply. It was universally understood that "from that" actually meant "from getting old."

G'ERTÁS G'ERTÁS CHı LıMıNNAR!

Կ'երթաս կ'երթաս չը լմննար

You go, you go, it never ends!

A common complaint when kids, (or great-grandmothers) have been sitting in the car too long and can't wait to reach the destination.

ERTALı KALı MEG EGHAV

Էրթալը գալը մէկ եղաւ

No sooner arrived, he left

Literally: "His coming and leaving became one."

This refers to a person who "understayed" their welcome and left too soon.

TEVERıS SANDAL ERI!

Թեւերս սանտալ ըրի

I've turned my arms into rowboats!

A common complaint when you've been doing all the work for everyone else.

Closest English equivalent: "Can't you see all I've done for you?"

SAPiTMISH EGHÁV!
Սափըրթմիշ Եղայ
It went haywire!

Turkish: *sapıtmış* = HAYWIRE

KHıZMET!

Խզմէթ

Housework! (Fate!)

The literal meaning of *Kismet* in Turkish is FORTUNE, or FATALITY. When household chores seemed never-ending and overwhelming, the elders of our family would exclaim loud enough for us to hear: *"Khısmet!"* as if to remind everyone that daily toil was their lot in life.

HELLÁK EGHÁ
Հեllաք Էղաj.
I'm exhausted

HOSDEGH MINCHEV YEP BEKLÈ'ENK BIDI?

Հոստեղ մինչեւ ե՞բ պեքլէենք պիտի

How long are we going to wait here?

Turk: *beklè* = WAIT. Arm: *...enk* = 1st person plural suffix

Beklè-enk bidi = WE ARE TO WAIT

For some reason, Acabi preferred the Turkish verb "*beklèmek*" to the Armenian verb "*ıspasel*" for WAIT. For her, the Turkish alternative better expressed her sense of frustration of having to wait too long. The rest of the phrase is entirely in Armenian, and the Turkish verb choice is conjugated in Armenian 1st person plural simple present suffix *-enk*.

INDZI TÁÁÁÁKH YOKHUSHIN TEPEN DARAV.

Ինձի թաաաաա՝խ եօխուշին թեփէն տարաւ

She took me 'waaaay' up to the top of the hill

Turkish: *yokush* can mean SLOPE, INCLINE, UPGRADE, or HILL; *Tepe* = PEAK, TOP.

Greek: *Taaaaakh (τααχ)* can be translated as SOOOO. It is basically an onomatopoeia for intensity or emphasis.

ASHKHARIN TÁÁÁÁKH ANTI-I DZARı DARAV!

Աշխարին թաաախ անդիի ծարը տարաւ

He took me 'waaay' to the other end of the world!

A complaint when someone took a painfully long, roundabout route to get somewhere. The *'taakh'* is the giveaway dialectical marker.

AD AL BAM Mı ıLLÁR!

Ադ ալ պամ մը ըլլար

Literally "May that, too, have been something!"

Western Armenian: *"Aïdnal pan mı ıllar."*

In other words, the object or situation in question is of no real importance.

The closest American English equivalent would be "BIG DEAL!"

Like many Mid-Eastern or West-Asian peoples, Armenians like to poke fun at people who take themselves or their accomplishments too seriously.

ALTıKH BEKLE'ELEN BıKHMISH EGHÁ

Ալտըխ պեկլէելէն պիսմիշ էղայ

I'm sick of waiting already!

Every word is Turkish, except "*eghá*," the first-person preterit of TO BE, which is the last word of the sentence.

Turk: *bıkmış* = FED UP; SICK OF... pronounced *bıkhmísh* in Acabi's Armenian.

INTERJECTIONS

KHELKÍS GUKAH!
Խելքիս կուգայ
I can't believe this!

As in "Are you kidding!"

Literally: "It's coming 'at' my mind!"

Khelk = MIND

KHENTENALÍK BAM Mı NÈ!
Խենթանալիք պամ մըն է
This is madness!

Literally: "This is something to drive you mad!"

Khent = CRAZY, MAD

KAVÚY!

Քա վույ

Wowww!

KHIYÁKH BAN!

Խիյախ պան

Big deal!

Khiyákh! = another way of saying WOW!, WOWWEE!!!

Literally: A "wowwee thing!" A sarcastic remark designed to take the wind out of someone's sails.

VAÏ VAÏ!!!
Վա՛յ վա՛յ
Well, get a load of this!

Vaï! = yet another form of WOW!

VAÏ AMBIDAN, VAÏ!

Վայ ամպիտան, վայ

You rascal, you!

Anbidan = BASTARD, S.O.B. -- but can also be used more lightly, as in "little rascal."

AMÁN DER ASDVADZ!
Աման տեր Աստվաձ
Oh my God!

Amán ! is a common interjection that could be interpreted as "Oh, my!"

Der Asdvadz = LORD GOD

OHÓ!!!
Ohoʹ
Goodness gracious! Wow!

AKH YÁ!
Ախ եա
Good grief!

BÁBAM!

Պապամ

For heaven's sake!

Although *Baba* means FATHER, the singular possessive *"M"* turns it into "MY FATHER!," used for emotional emphasis among peers.

ÖFF BÈ!
Èo`ֆ այէ
Enough already!

Turkish: *Öff!* = PFFF !!; UGH !!

An onomatopoeia expressing one's frustration with an ongoing situation.

HAÏDÈ! / HADDÈ
Հայդէ, հատտէ
Come on, let's go!

(Istanbul dialect)

It can also be used in the sense of "Hurry up!"

EXPRESSIONS

OF

ENDEARMENT

EVLADıM

Էվլատըմ

My child, my boy

Arabic: *el walad* = Turkish: *evlad* = CHILD

MANTCHıS
մանչս
My child

DGHAS

տղաս

My boy

AGHTCHIGıS

աղջիկս

My daughter, my girl

HOKIS IMIN!
Հոգիս իմին
My sweetheart!

Armenian, literally: MY SOUL

YÁVRUS!
Եավրուս
My baby!

Turkish:

Yavru = BABY + Armenian possessive suffix - */s/

TSÁKıS!

Ձագս

My little one!

Armenian: *tsak*, or *dzak* = CUB, CHICK, PUPPY, CALF or any newborn OFFSPRING

ANUSHÍGıS
Անուշիկս
My sweet one!

Armenian: *anush* = SWEET, + *-ig* = diminutive
anushig = LITTLE SWEETIE

ANUSH SHEKER ıLLÁ
Անուշ շեքեր ըլլայ
Enjoy!

For food.

Literally: "May it be sugar sweet!"

BOYıT BOSSıT SIREM!

Պոյդ պoսդ սիրեմ

I love seeing you grow!

PRONUNCIATION GUIDE

The words and expressions in this book are transcribed in two alphabets, Armenian and Roman letters.

As a general rule of pronunciation, stress falls on the final syllable of words in both Turkish and Armenian, except for certain loan words from other languages.

ENGLISH LETTERS

Every Armenian word has been transliterated into Roman letters, as well as Armenian letters.

The consonant '**G**' is to be pronounced always as a hard G, as in GATE.

The digraph '**GH**' is a guttural R, such as the Parisian R.

The digraph '**KH**' is pronounced like the 'ch,' as in Scottish LO<u>CH</u>.

The letter 'A' is to be pronounced like the A in FATHER.

(Just to facilitate things, I place an accent over the Á whenever the syllable is accentuated.)

The letter 'I' is to be pronounced as /EE/ in SLEEP. I also place an accent over the Í when the syllable is accentuated.

The letter 'E', for which I often use the French grave accent È at the end of a word, is to be pronounced like the E in BED. However, it is not necessarily an accentuated syllable.

The letter 'U' is pronounced as /OO/ in FOOD, MOON, or GOOFY. (In certain cases I have used the double 'OO' simply for its visual effect.)

Aside from the vowels listed above, all other vowels and diphthongs correspond roughly to their equivalent pronunciation in English.

As for the "Schwa" sound, designated by the symbol /ə/ in the English phonetic alphabet, I have used the Turkish undotted 'I' = ı

The Schwa sound is common in both English, Turkish and Armenian. It is a short vowel sound, barely uttered, without opening the mouth very wide. It sounds like the /a/ in **a**side; like the /e/ in moth**er**; it is the first and last vowel in the word **A**meric**a** = /əmerikə/.

Since the Armenian letter /ը/ and the Turkish /ı/ are pronounced almost identically, I have chosen to use, for simplicity's sake, the Turkish letter /ı/ instead of the phonetic symbol /ə/ or the Armenian /ը/.

ARMENIAN ALPHABET: CONSONANTS

For words spelled in Armenian letters, consonants are to be pronounced as in WESTERN ARMENIAN. For example, the consonants բ-գ-դ-պ-ք are to be pronounced as follows:

/**բ**/ => /p/ as in 'Paul'

/**գ**/ => /k/ as in 'cake'

/**դ**/ => /t/ as in 'take

/** պ**/ => /g/ as in 'game'

/** պ**/ => /b/ as in 'boy'

/**ջ**/ => /ch/ as in 'church'

/**դ**/ => /d/ as in 'Daniel'

ONLINE RESOURCES

You can listen to the correct pronunciation of each sentence online by visiting the following link:

https://bit.ly/m/acabisarmenian

or by scanning this QR code:

ACKNOWLEDGEMENTS

Deepest thanks to **Haig Avakian** who dared break the official spelling rules in order to "spell it as it is" in his Armenian alphabet transliterations.

Thanks also to **Roubina Tabakian** for her input with the Konya dialect.

Edwin Gerard Hamamdjian was born in Los Angeles, California in 1948. After graduating from UCLA and earning a Master's in French literature at UC Berkeley, he moved to France where he obtained a Doctorate in Theatre Arts at the Université de Paris 3, Sorbonne Nouvelle. As an award-winning director, playwright and actor, he has worked extensively in the US, France, Italy, and India. He has taught in the theatre department of USC, UCLA, University of Paris 8, as well as in various private acting schools. He is fluent in several European and Near Eastern languages. Edwin currently resides in Cairo, Egypt where he is studying Arabic.

Nadia Brugnara is an illustrator and 2D animator living in Paris, France. Born in 1986 in a small village in the Italian Alps, she grew up speaking the local dialect, fostering a strong connection to her roots. After earning her degree in Animation in Florence, she worked on several Italian and international animated TV shows as an animator and a storyboard artist. Her career has taken her across different countries, fueling her passion for both storytelling and learning new languages.